CAPTURED
TELEVISION
HISTORY

TV EXPOSES BRUTALITY ON
THE SELMA MARCH

An Augmented Reading Experience

D1306812

By Danielle Smith-Llera

Content Adviser: Alan Schroeder, Professor,
School of Journalism, Northeastern University

COMPASS POINT BOOKS
a capstone imprint

Compass Point Books are published by Capstone Press,
1710 Roe Crest Drive, North Mankato, Minnesota 56003
www.capstonepub.com

Editorial Credits
Michelle Bisson, editor; Tracy McCabe, designer; Svetlana Zhurkin, media researcher;
Katy LaVigne, production specialist

Photo Credits
Alabama Department of Archives and History/Donated by the Alabama Media Group/Birmingham News:
Ed Jones, 9, 31, 33, 34, 58 (top), Ed Jones or Robert Adams, 27, Elizabeth Boone Aiken, 7, 11, Haywood Paravicini, 45, 59 (top right), Tom Lankford, 5, 13, 44, Tom Self or Anthony Falletta, 49, 58 (bottom left); AP Photo: 24, Horace Cort, 36, 40, Jack Thornell, 15, The Herald-Times/Jeremy Hogan, 51; Getty Images: Bettmann, 38, 47, Express/William Lovelace, 53; The Image Works: TopFoto, 42; LBJ Library photo by Yoichi Okamoto, 58 (bottom right); Library of Congress, cover, 21, 29, 56, 57, 59 (top left); Newscom: Everett Collection, 23, 26, Zuma Press/Marvin J. Wolf, 16; Official White House photo by Lawrence Jackson, 55, 59 (bottom); Shutterstock: Everett Historical, 19, 20

Library of Congress Cataloging-in-Publication Data
Names: Smith-Llera, Danielle, 1971- author.
Title: TV exposes brutality on the Selma March : 4D, an augmented reading
experience / by Danielle Smith-Llera.
Other titles: Television exposes brutality on the Selma March Description: North Mankato, Minnesota:
Compass Point Books, [2020] | Series: Captured television history 4D | Audience: Ages: 10 to 12. |
Audience: Grades: 4 to 6. | Includes bibliographical references and index.
Identifiers: LCCN 2018054585| ISBN 9780756560010 (hardcover)
ISBN 9780756560058 (pbk.) | ISBN 9780756560096 (ebook PDF)
Subjects: LCSH: Selma to Montgomery Rights March (1965 : Selma, Ala.)—Juvenile literature. | Civil rights demonstrations—Alabama—History—20th century—Juvenile literature. |
Television and politics—United States—History—20th century—Juvenile literature. | Violence-—
Press coverage—United States—History—20th century—Juvenile literature. | African Americans—
Civil rights—Southern States—History—20th century—Juvenile literature. | Southern States—Race relations—History—20th century—Juvenile literature.
Classification: LCC F334.S4 S65 2020 | DDC 323.1196/073075—dc23
LC record available at https://lccn.loc.gov/2018054585

All internet sites appearing in back matter were available and accurate when this book was sent to press.

Download the Capstone app!

- Ask an adult to download the Capstone 4D app.

- Scan the cover and stars inside the book for additional content.

When you scan a spread, you'll find fun extra stuff to go with this book! You can also find these things on the web at www.capstone4D.com using the password: selma.60010

Printed and bound in the United States of America.
PA70

TABLE OF CONTENTS

ChapterOne
ALL EYES ON THE BRIDGE

Around 48 million Americans were wrapping up their weekend on Sunday night, March 7, 1965, by watching an award-winning movie on ABC TV. But at 9:30 p.m. Eastern Standard Time the evening took an unexpected turn. News anchor Frank Reynolds interrupted the movie with a news broadcast. ABC network executives had decided this news could not wait. It was considered as important as the assassination of a president or a space launch, both of which had interrupted television programming in recent years. Reynolds briefly introduced an event that took place in Selma, a small town in central Alabama, earlier that day. Viewers then watched 15 minutes of footage that left them stunned.

Hours earlier, a quiet scene had unfolded on a cool spring day in Selma. Two men stepped onto a steel bridge, walking side by side along the narrow walkway, their hands tucked into the pockets of their buttoned coats. Below them, the Alabama River flowed in its zigzagging path between Selma and the state capital of Montgomery. But black activists Hosea Williams and John Lewis were not on a lazy weekend stroll this Sunday afternoon. They were headed to Montgomery. The Edmund Pettus Bridge and then Interstate 80 could get cars and buses there in about

TV viewers saw scenes such as this one—two marchers holding up another brutally injured in the police attack at the Edmund Pettus Bridge.

an hour. But the men had an astonishing plan. They would travel the 54 miles (87 kilometers) on foot—a journey that would take days.

Television crews and cameras waited at the other end of the arched bridge to capture this unusual event—particularly since, behind Williams and Lewis, an orderly column of about 600 people was also headed toward Montgomery. Lewis later recalled the unnatural quiet of the massive procession moving in two single-file lines. Black men, women, and children as young as 8 years old from Selma and the surrounding Dallas County marched up the steep bridge. "There was no singing, no shouting— just the sound of scuffling feet . . . the marching feet of a determined people. That was the only sound you could hear," recalled Lewis. But their calm faces masked rage. It had been a century since the 13th constitutional amendment had outlawed slavery, yet many black citizens found they still did not enjoy the same rights as white citizens. It had been a decade since the U.S. Supreme Court outlawed the segregation of black people from white people in public schools—yet some schools still resisted admitting black students. It had been a year since the Supreme Court outlawed segregation in all public places, but black citizens felt that the greatest right of all was still out of reach.

In Selma and across the South, black citizens were blocked from participating in the nation's democracy. Half of Dallas County's 30,000 residents were black, but just 4 percent of them were registered to vote. When they went to Selma's courthouse to register, black residents were usually ignored and left to wait for hours. If they were eventually called up to the registrar's desk, they had to take a literacy test. But they were not given the same easy tests as white applicants. The tests for black applicants ranged from overly complicated

"There was no singing, no shouting— just . . . the marching feet of a determined people."

to outrageous. They might be asked to write long passages from the state constitution or to guess the number of jelly beans in a jar. "DENIED" was usually stamped on their applications.

Young people led the voting rights movement in the South.

The consequences of trying to register could be severe. White employers fired black employees who tried to register to vote. Banks stopped lending money to black applicants, which meant they could lose their homes and businesses. Applicants even faced brutal assaults by local white people. Still, many activists believed it was worth risking everything for the right to vote. The marchers heading over the bridge were on their way to Montgomery to see Alabama governor George Wallace and demand their right as U.S. citizens to become registered voters.

When the marchers reached the bridge, they had traveled less than a mile from where they had gathered at Selma's Brown Chapel. But their journey had started long before. Famous civil rights leader Martin Luther King Jr. had visited Brown Chapel on January 2. He stood at the pulpit to announce an ambitious plan. He invited listeners to join a campaign to help everyone in Alabama exercise their right to vote.

In the two months following, activists did indeed join this "Give us the ballot!" campaign. They had gathered at Brown Chapel to march to the courthouse together in groups of more than 100.

Sheriff Jim Clark oversaw the courthouse in Selma. He wore a military-style jacket, a belt usually holding a pistol, a club and a cattle prod, and a button pinned to his uniform to remind protesters of his

Brown Chapel was a meeting place for civil rights events. The renewed voter registration drive was kicked off there.

stance on equal voting rights. It read, "Never." He had used his fist, his club, and his band of undisciplined armed deputies against the protesters. Clark made the courthouse a dangerous place.

But as the protesters walked away from Selma, Williams felt exhilarated. He later recalled it as "one of the most gratifying and most memorable moments of my whole life. I don't think I [have] ever seen Americans more ready and willing to suffer and sacrifice for dignity, for human dignity, in my whole life," he recalled. "And I was just . . . so happy to see all of those people . . ." But within minutes this joy would be replaced by the terrifying thought, "Oh my god, how many people did I lead to their death today?"

As the marchers crossed the bridge, Lewis looked grimly ahead. The march was "somber and subdued, almost like a funeral procession," he later recalled. He assumed the marchers would be arrested before they ever reached Montgomery. He wore a backpack that contained food and books—not for a long march—but for a stay in jail. After all, Governor Wallace had forbidden the march. Wallace had instructed Alabama state troopers—with help from Clark's men—to stop the marchers by any means. More than 200 armed men blocked the road that stretched all the way to Montgomery. Rows of Alabama state troopers waited under the command of Major John Cloud. Behind them stood Clark and his men, some on horseback and hefting clubs. Waving Confederate flags at the roadside, dozens of white people cheered eagerly for a showdown with the marchers.

Another group of white men had been watching the marchers cross the bridge. They were armed too—but with notepads and pens, cameras and sound equipment. For Sheriff Clark and Major Cloud, these tools made them dangerous witnesses to what was about to happen. Four troopers were posted to confine

"Your march is not conducive to the public safety. You are ordered to disperse and go back to your church or to your homes."

Sheriff Jim Clark (right) gave permission to a number of white men to use violence against protesters. He even supplied the clubs and hard hats.

the reporters and photographers to a parking lot about 100 yards away from the foot of the bridge. But these experienced journalists would get their story. Like civil rights activists, they had learned how to do their work even when laws and hostile police stood in their way.

When just 50 feet (15 meters) separated the unarmed marchers and the armed men, Cloud raised a bullhorn and his voice boomed out, "This is an unlawful assembly. Your march is not conducive to the public safety. You are ordered to disperse and go back to your church or to your homes." But the procession was too long to allow a quick retreat. And it was too dangerous for the marchers to advance closer to the armed men, some wearing tear gas masks as if prepared for war. Lewis told Williams,

"We should kneel and pray." But as the first marchers began to drop down with bowed heads, Cloud shouted an order to his men: "Troopers, advance!" Rows of armed men shot forward with clubs raised.

A trooper struck Lewis on the head. He fell to the ground and the club struck again. He lay with a fractured skull as the scene wheeled dizzily around him. Tear gas exploded out of canisters and the toxic, gray cloud choked Lewis. He thought, "People are going to die here. I'm going to die here." Around Lewis, marchers wept and bled, vomiting from the tear gas. He saw Clark's men ride their horses over the bodies of fallen people, swinging whips, clubs, and electric cattle prods. Lying nearby, another march leader sprawled in deathlike stillness where a state trooper had beaten her. Fifty-three-year-old activist Amelia Boynton had been fighting for voting rights in Dallas County since the 1930s. Marchers carried her back to Brown Chapel, where hundreds retreated in a panic. Lewis made it back too. By the end of the day as many as 70 marchers were injured, with at least 17 hospitalized.

No one died on the day that became known as "Bloody Sunday." But the images that day produced what would be the most dramatic filmed coverage of a protest in civil rights history. Even marchers themselves would need to see the footage to understand what happened.

A state trooper stood over Amelia Boynton after she was attacked during the march.

After losing consciousness, Boynton didn't "remember anything else, except the pictures that I saw and what was told to me." It was the work of the group of cameramen peering into the tear gas and chaos to tell the marchers, the nation, and the world what had happened.

But as they filmed, cameramen could not be sure what their cameras were capturing. Before video cameras, film had to be developed in chemicals for cameramen to be able to see it. Just a piece of dirt or a hair on the camera could cast a shadow on the film that would make it unacceptable for broadcast. CBS cameraman Laurens Pierce was at the bridge that day. He was worried about his work, saying "I think I got it. I mean I hope I got it. I feel like I got it."

The national television camera crews raced to catch rides to Montgomery, where they used the darkrooms and chemical baths at local television stations to develop the film. The images on the film strips could be viewed once they were projected onto a screen. Packed into round canisters, the developed film traveled by plane to the New York City headquarters of TV networks. Editors and producers viewed the film to decide what to show and when to show it. CBS and NBC wasted little time in broadcasting it on the Sunday evening news.

In his Selma hotel room that night, newspaper reporter Roy Reed of *The New York Times* watched on TV the event he had witnessed with his own eyes at the bridge. Pierce's skill and bravery awed him. He had gotten closer than any other cameraman to the violence with his bulky camera. CBS correspondent Nelson Benton presented just 3 minutes, 15 seconds of footage. It began with the camera moving between the approaching marchers and the wall of waiting law enforcement. It ended with screams as parked cars and tear gas blocked the horror. "There was no way print could capture the drama and the vicious

RISKY BUSINESS

Laurens Pierce (left) was punched in the face by Alton Roberts, who was later sentenced in connection with the deaths of three civil rights workers in 1964.

Decades before cable television and the internet offered news 24 hours a day, millions of viewers depended on an evening news report for the day's news. Television anchors such as CBS's Walter Cronkite were familiar faces to Americans. But far from well-lit studios, cameramen such as Laurens Pierce did unglamorous but critical work. Since the mid–1950s Pierce had traveled around the South filming protests, speeches, and violence that told the story of the hard struggle of black citizens for equal rights. Yet his name and face were not familiar to viewers watching what he filmed on Bloody Sunday.

Work was dangerous for cameramen like Pierce. With glasses usually pushed up into his hair so he could peer through his lens, he was willing to charge into the most dangerous situations with his large camera. John Lewis explained that journalists covering the civil rights struggle "all faced danger, especially the TV guys, who were easily identified and easy targets because of their equipment. The print reporters could blend in with a crowd if they had to, but the TV cameramen, guys like La[urens] Pierce with CBS, were right out front." Pierce adapted to these dangers: He added a detachable bar to his camera equipment that he could use to defend himself. "Pierce, in particular, is a man I will never forget," Lewis wrote. "A lot of the civil rights scenes America saw each evening back then, with Walter Cronkite narrating, were footage shot by Pierce."

attack on the demonstrators on Bloody Sunday the way TV did," NBC correspondent Richard Valeriani later said. "I put it on the air with hardly any narrative. I said something like, 'Civil rights activists demonstrating for voting rights tried to march from Selma to Montgomery today but were stopped by Alabama state troopers. Here's what happened.'"

That evening, TV viewers across the nation watched the chaos in Selma from their living rooms. In eastern Alabama, student activist Gwen Patton watched on a dormitory TV set with fellow activists at all-black Tuskegee University. She had fought for voting rights since the age of 16. The students had already staged local demonstrations supported by the Student Nonviolent Coordinating Committee (SNCC), but what they saw on television led them to head

Photographers and cameramen waited for the protesters to try to march to Montgomery again, two days after the events of Bloody Sunday.

"When Bloody Sunday was televised all over the country, today you would say it went viral."

straight for the state capital themselves. We've "got to really gear up, get our stuff organized, organize the community, get cars," Patton remembered students saying as they made the hasty plan. "We're going to Montgomery!" At the capital they would stage protests and face attacks by police officers.

Many more people who saw the Bloody Sunday broadcasts lived hundreds, even thousands, of miles away. Many were not black. Still, some felt a strong urge to take action. One was George Leonard, a journalist watching the news from California, who remembered "a shrill cry of terror, unlike any sound that had passed through a TV set" as the attack began. When tear gas blocked the view of the violence, the screams and glimpses of helmets and swinging clubs told viewers what was happening inside the tear gas cloud. "Unhuman. No other word can describe the motions," Leonard later wrote. He and his wife boarded a plane to Selma that night, as did many others from cities across the nation.

"When Bloody Sunday was televised all over the country, today you would say it went viral. It was sort of like after 9/11," Claire Wahrhaftig remembered. Soon hundreds of TV viewers would stand shoulder to shoulder with the marchers they had seen on TV. They would set out on a second march across the Edmund Pettus Bridge, where armed men would be waiting once again.

Chapter Two

MARCHES MADE FOR TELEVISION

"I gave a little blood on the bridge, but some people gave their lives," Lewis told a group of young leaders gathered at the White House in 2016. "The vote is precious. It is the most powerful nonviolent tool we have in a democratic society, and we must use it." The sacrifices on the Edmund Pettus Bridge were part of a long struggle against injustice and brutality.

Kidnapped from Africa, black people were enslaved and sold to white people who forced them to work under brutal conditions for almost 250 years. They earned no pay and had no rights since they were considered property, not human beings. Life in the southern states depended on slavery to raise profitable crops like cotton. This was a major reason why, in 1861, Alabama decided to join the Confederacy of southern states and declare independence from the northern states that had abolished slavery. Southern states lost the Civil War and 4 million black people were freed. To rejoin the Union, war-torn southern states had to accept new federal laws. One was the 13th Amendment, which, in 1865, made slavery illegal in every state of the nation. The 14th Amendment, in 1868, went further. It promised black people citizenship and the same protections under U.S. laws as white people had.

Union forces liberated enslaved people from a South Carolina plantation in 1861.

In 1870 the 15th Amendment guaranteed the right of male black citizens to vote. (No woman, white or black, could vote in presidential elections until the 19th Amendment was passed in 1920.) Results came quickly. More than half a million new black voters helped elect as many as 2,000 black candidates as city councilmen, mayors, sheriffs, and state lawmakers across the nation. More than a dozen went to Washington, D.C., to serve in Congress.

When Senator Hiram Revels of Mississippi was elected in 1871 as the first black member of Congress, he was called the "15th Amendment in flesh and blood." But after the federal government removed troops from former Confederate states in 1877, voting grew increasingly dangerous for black citizens in the South. Bands of white racists such as the Ku Klux Klan terrorized and murdered black people who were exercising new freedoms. Meanwhile, white voters filled southern state governments with members of the all-white Democratic Party that had supported slavery and the Confederacy. State leaders appointed registrars who administered the ruthless literacy tests. They also passed laws requiring applicants to pay a poll tax and own property. At the same time, they passed other laws that allowed many white, illiterate men without property to vote.

Hiram Revels

Black citizens lost the power to influence laws. From the 1880s onward, white lawmakers in state and local governments across the South and elsewhere in the U.S. passed laws that forced black and white people to live separately. These so-called Jim Crow laws meant that black people could not attend the same schools or use the same restaurants, bathrooms, or even drinking fountains. The facilities they had to use were inferior, or sometimes nonexistent. For example, gas stations might have restrooms for white people but none for those who were black.

In 1944, a decade before the Supreme Court ruled that segregation in public schools was

Jim Crow laws meant that many facilities were segregated throughout the South.

unconstitutional, voting activists won a major victory. In *Smith v. Allwright,* the Court ruled that it was unconstitutional for the Democratic Party in some southern states to bar black voters from voting in primary elections. Lead lawyer and future Supreme Court Justice Thurgood Marshall explained the power of this decision: "Without the ballot, you have no citizenship, no status, no power in this country." Marshall would go on to convince the Court that segregation in public schools is unconstitutional in the 1954 case *Brown v. Board of Education of Topeka.*

Congress passed the first civil rights laws in almost a century in 1957 and 1960. But they did nothing about poll taxes or literacy tests. While they called for anyone restricting voting to be tried in federal courts, cases piled up at a pace faster than judges could hear them. And even when the cases were heard, judges did not generally rule for those protesting the law.

How could black citizens without the power to vote change unjust laws? When the vote is denied, it leaves people no choice but to resist. Lewis's advice is to "get in trouble, what I call good trouble, necessary trouble." Black activists had witnessed the success of Mahatma Gandhi's mass march in 1930. For nearly a century, Great Britain ruled over most of its colony of India with harsh laws. One placed a high tax on salt and even outlawed collecting it on beaches. Gandhi set out on a three-week march across 240 miles (386 km). Gandhi led thousands of marchers to the shore of the Arabian Sea to do just that: collect salt. Gandhi inspired others across the colony to break this unjust law. Within weeks, 80,000 were arrested, many beaten by police. Millions around the world saw black-and-white recordings of the Salt March thanks to three film crews from Mumbai. Some black U.S. citizens responded to this march in a personal way.

Gandhi's Salt March proved that large-scale, peaceful demonstrations could grab the world's attention—with the help of journalists and cameras. Black church leaders and professors in the U.S. began to spread this idea to young activists.

". . . get in trouble, what I call good trouble, necessary trouble."

Activist Mahatma Gandhi (center) led the Salt March to the Arabian Sea.

Civil rights leader A. Philip Randolph planned a march of 10,000 black activists in the nation's capital to protest segregation in the military. The threat of this massive march was enough to intimidate even a U.S. president. To avoid the 1941 march, President Franklin Roosevelt negotiated with activists.

A massive protest began quietly on a segregated bus in Montgomery, Alabama, in December 1955. Activist Rosa Parks refused to give up her seat to a white passenger. She and other community leaders, including Martin Luther King Jr., organized as many as 40,000 black citizens of Montgomery to boycott city buses. After the yearlong protest, a federal court ruled that segregated city buses were unconstitutional. Soon after, King and black church leaders from 10 states formed the Southern Christian Leadership Conference (SCLC). The SCLC helped teach techniques of nonviolent protest.

At age 15 John Lewis heard King speak on the radio during the bus boycott. "And I felt like he was talking to me," Lewis remembered years later. As a college student in Nashville, Tennessee, Lewis was inspired by King's example to lead nonviolent protests. The protesters sat down at lunch counters reserved for white people, ordered food, were refused,

Two black men sit in the first seat of a Montgomery bus. The bus boycott led to the end of segregation on city buses.

"Television pictures of recurring horrors such as the attacks that bloodied Freedom Riders . . . had become nightly fare."

but didn't leave. During these sit-ins, students endured insults and attacks with food and fists. Yet protesters stayed calm when faced with unruly white opponents in cities across the United States. Young protesters representing 12 southern states formed SNCC in April 1960.

A bus in Anniston, Alabama, was deliberately set on fire on May 14, 1961. Dazed passengers barely escaped. The targets of the fire were Freedom Riders—black and white activists testing whether bus station lunch counters, waiting rooms, and bathrooms were still segregated after the Supreme Court ruled the practice unconstitutional in 1956. Another bus reached Birmingham's bus station, where police allowed white attackers to savagely beat activists. One needed 53 stitches. Images of this brutality pressured President John F. Kennedy to send federal forces to escort buses out of Alabama. "Television pictures of recurring horrors such as the attacks that bloodied Freedom Riders . . . had become nightly fare," wrote TV journalist Howard K. Smith, "Even indifferent citizens were beginning to feel and to say, 'Something must be done.'"

Activists launched an ambitious plan in late 1961 to desegregate the city of Albany, Georgia—but King declared it a failure. Police Chief Laurie Pritchett made sure his men arrested protesters with care. "We knew their theory was nonviolence, so we base

Freedom Riders barely escaped a fire set by those who opposed their mission.

our theory on nonviolence also. This has stunned them. They were expecting police brutality." Like Sheriff Jim Clark, Pritchett believed firmly in segregation. But unlike Clark, Pritchett understood that images of police attacking protesters would portray the police as evil.

Birmingham's openly racist commissioner of public safety, Bull Connor, did not understand that, or didn't care. He had bragged to a *New York Times* reporter, "Down here we make our own law."

Protesters marched to the county building to register to vote on May 3, 1963. Connor made the event world news when he instructed police to attack them with dogs and blasts from high-pressure fire

Commissioner of Public Safety Bull Connor personally ordered the brutal police action against the Selma marchers.

hoses. Local white-owned newspapers did not publish photographs of the police brutality at first. But national TV crews broadcast disturbing scenes, such as a police officer kicking down a protester so a dog could pounce. The nation watched black protesters bravely face violence, even singing in defiance. Many Americans were shocked. In a televised address on June 11, 1963, President Kennedy promised to urge Congress to pass new civil rights laws.

Two months later, 250,000 demonstrators in Washington, D.C., marched in support of a new civil rights bill struggling through Congress. Television cameras broadcast live to worldwide audiences on August 28, 1963, courtesy of new satellite technology.

Television crews told a joyful story of racial harmony. They zoomed in on close-ups of black and white protesters walking together. They broadcast King delivering his famous "I Have a Dream" speech. But CBS, the network to broadcast longest from the march, did not cover John Lewis's speech, which, unlike King's, was not hopeful. "As it stands now," he said, "the voting section of this bill will not help the thousands of people who want to vote. It will not help the citizens of Mississippi, of Alabama and Georgia, who are unqualified to vote for lack of a sixth grade education."

The following summer, the Civil Rights Act of 1964 finally became law. Lyndon Johnson had become president after President Kennedy was assassinated on November 22, 1963. Johnson, though a southerner, energetically pushed the bill. Besides banning segregation, the new Civil Rights Act stated that voting requirements must be identical for all applicants. But without banning literacy tests and poll taxes, the new law could not be enforced.

That summer civil rights organizations were busy in Mississippi, the state with the country's lowest percentage of black voters. Mississippi activists and hundreds of white college students from the North knocked on doors, urging black residents to register. Leaders hoped to attract media attention and federal protection to the cause. After all, voting activists had

A NEW PARTY

MFDP supporters held signs in front of the convention hall reading "One man, one vote, MFDP."

Black southerners were not allowed to participate in the Democratic Party's presidential primary election. So SNCC founded the Mississippi Freedom Democratic Party (MFDP) in April 1964. It was open to anyone of any race, and 80,000 black Mississippi residents joined. They brought 68 delegates to the all-white national Democratic National Convention in Atlantic City, New Jersey, in August. They demanded to be part of the process of electing the Democratic presidential candidate.

On TV, SNCC activist Fannie Lou Hamer declared, "If the Mississippi Freedom Democratic Party is not seated now, I question America. Is this America? The land of the free and the home of the brave where we [are] threatened daily because we want to live as decent human beings in America?" She wept as she described assaults at civil rights rallies. President Johnson hastily called a press conference to draw television coverage away from her. But that night, television news broadcast Hamer's full speech.

The next day, Johnson arranged for two seats to be offered to MFDP delegates. Hamer refused. She called them "token seats, in the back row, the same as we got in Mississippi. We didn't come all this way for that mess again." But the experience proved the power of regular citizens to organize into a powerful force.

been murdered in broad daylight for years without investigations or arrests. But the federal government offered no help even though Freedom Summer volunteers faced arrests, attacks, and bombs in houses where they stayed. National television news closely followed the story of three volunteers, two white and one black—Andrew Goodman, Michael Schwerner, and James Chaney—who were murdered by Ku Klux Klan members. Many younger activists questioned the power of nonviolence in the face of such brutality.

But King had seen how effective nonviolent protests were in desegregating the bus system in Birmingham. In November 1964 activists invited King to launch a voting campaign in Selma, Alabama. Local voting activists and SNCC members had already staged a bold public protest there in 1963. CBS cameraman Wendell Hoffman was among the journalists gathered at the courthouse on October 7, or "Freedom Day."

More than 350 protesters waited in line to register for hours. Sheriff Clark, in a helmet stamped with a Confederate flag, forbade anyone from bringing them food or water. Two SNCC members brought food and drink to the weary protesters anyway. State troopers kicked and attacked both men with clubs and cattle prods. An officer ordered his men to block the cameramen's view. Using his camera as a shield, Hoffman protected himself from the troopers' blows.

Hundreds of protesters gathered at the Dallas County courthouse on Freedom Day.

Yet protesters celebrated Freedom Day as a great success. Clark—and the nation—had witnessed hundreds of black citizens overcome fear to stand in the registration line. But standing in line wasn't enough. Black citizens were still being denied the right to register—and to vote.

ChapterThree
WATCHING FROM HOME, TAKING SIDES

King drove to Selma from Atlanta to announce the launch of the SCLC–organized Selma voting campaign. He found about 700 people waiting for him inside Brown Chapel on January 2, 1965, including Lewis and Williams. All eyes were on King as he stood at the pulpit. They were not asking to vote, he reminded them. They were demanding the vote. He assured his listeners that together they could make history. Selma's campaign would force the federal government to ensure their right to vote. Everywhere King went, cameras followed and the world watched.

King expected violence against the protesters in Alabama, and he wanted television cameras to be there. King knew the power of television to draw viewers into a story. He vowed to bring the violence faced by black people to the nation's attention through unforgettable images. After all, by 1965 Americans were increasingly tuning into nightly television news reports with on-location sound and visuals.

SNCC activists had been pushing for the vote in Selma since 1962. They had seen proof that Sheriff Clark's violent reactions guaranteed a spot for Selma in the nightly television news report: "Sheriff Jim

Student marchers in Selma, Alabama, protested efforts to prevent voter registration.

Clark was a big man," recalled John Lewis. "Big hat, big man, nightstick. And a lot of people were afraid of him, not just black citizens but also white citizens." In short, he was a perfect enemy for those struggling to attain the right to vote.

Two weeks after King's announcement, activists began marching almost daily from Brown Chapel to the courthouse as protesters had on Freedom Day in 1963. But the new campaign did not seem likely to produce the televised violence that stunned the nation in Birmingham—at first. One obstacle was Selma's public safety director, Wilson Baker. He understood

Sheriff Clark used violence against activist C.T. Vivian on the courthouse steps.

that without violence captured on camera, the nation—and the federal government—would not be interested in the voting campaign. Baker allowed marchers to proceed or arrested them without violence. His men kept white opponents at a distance and arrested them if they attacked.

Despite Baker's restraint, Clark behaved as predicted. Television viewers watched him grab longtime activist Amelia Boynton by the collar and drag her from the courthouse to a police car a block away. Cameras made the violent arrest national news. Yet days later, Clark and his deputies roughly pushed a large group of Selma's black teachers down the courthouse steps. When 161 teenagers skipped school to gather at the courthouse with signs reading "Let Our Parents Vote," Clark and his deputies forced them to run out of the city, where they attacked the teens with clubs and cattle prods. Clark denied the violence, and television cameras were too far away to prove he was lying. TV cameras did capture Clark punching activist C.T. Vivian in the mouth so hard that he broke his own hand doing so.

King had another strategy for attracting cameras and national attention to the campaign. He marched to the courthouse with hundreds of supporters on February 1, hoping to go to jail. The plan worked. Television viewers saw Baker arrest the world-famous activist, and Congress members arranged to meet with King. President Johnson pledged his support for Selma activists in a press conference. *The New York Times*, on February 5, published King's letter about his stay in the Selma jail. He grimly joked that there were more black people in jail with him than on the city's voting rolls. The next day, a federal government spokesman made a long-awaited announcement: President Johnson would pressure Congress to pass a voting rights bill.

But activists knew they would have to apply pressure to make new voting laws a reality. Two thousand protesters packed Selma's jail. Not a single

A group of about 300 demonstrators were arrested and taken to a nearby jail after marching on the Perry County courthouse.

one had successfully registered to vote.

A tragedy in Marion, a town about 30 miles (48 km) from Selma, dramatically changed the course of the Selma movement—even though television camera crews tried, but failed, to record exactly what happened. About 450 people set out from their church on the night of February 18, 1965. They marched toward the jail to sing inspiring songs to an SCLC activist who had been arrested while organizing voting drives. About 200 police officers and state troopers in riot gear waited, expecting the protesters to break into the jail. Clark was there too, even though Marion was not part of his territory. A reporter asked him, "Don't you have enough trouble of your own in Selma?" Clark replied, "Things got a little too quiet for me." Marion's police chief ordered the marchers back. When they knelt to pray, state troopers attacked.

Someone sprayed CBS cameraman Bernie Nudelman's lens with paint. He wiped it away and tried to keep filming. But the streetlights flickered out. TV crews turned on camera lights, but police ordered them turned off. In the darkness, townspeople and police beat the unarmed protesters. Then gunshots rang out. State trooper James Bonard Fowler had shot 26-year-old Jimmie Lee Jackson in the stomach as he protected his mother. The young activist would die of the wound eight days later. He had not succeeded in registering to vote in his short lifetime. But his murder would drive the voting rights movement forward with unstoppable power.

TV viewers saw the dim and choppy films from Marion. It was clear that the situation was out of control, despite what police claimed. CBS correspondent Bill Plante reported that a deputy sheriff had said, "It was a small incident. One Negro fell down." Television crews were determined to tell the brutal story some locals and the police wanted to avoid. NBC correspondent Richard Valeriani even delivered his TV news report from a hospital bed after a white local beat him with an ax handle that night.

Outraged activists vowed to carry Jackson's coffin

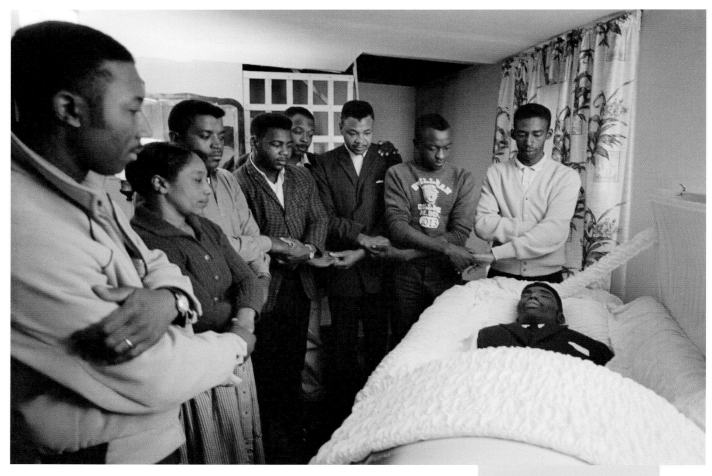

to Governor George Wallace himself, depositing it on the steps of the Montgomery Capitol. But SCLC activist James Bevel urged the audience at Jackson's memorial service on February 26 to use the power of a massive protest instead. "The blood of Jackson will be on our hands if we don't march," Bevel said. "Be prepared to walk to Montgomery. Be prepared to sleep on the highways."

King planned to lead this march, guaranteeing cameras would be rolling. Danger and violence

"The blood of Jackson will be on our hands if we don't march. Be prepared to walk to Montgomery. Be prepared to sleep on the highways."

followed him everywhere, whether it was police or white mobs attacking demonstrators or the possibility someone would assassinate him. Newspeople depended on King to deliver what kept viewers tuned to their stations: drama. And these viewers meant profits. Television networks charged advertisers to broadcast commercials to potential customers. The more people watched their network, the more networks could charge advertisers.

News programs were hungry for fresh news to broadcast every night. Even with Jackson's death, the Selma campaign was mentioned only three times on NBC news shows during the following two weeks. The protest organizers feared that TV producers were losing interest in the Selma campaign. A massive march was a chance to get Selma back in the national spotlight. This time it would be on the bridge named in 1940 after Edmund Pettus—a U.S. senator who had also been a Ku Klux Klan leader.

Adding to the tension on March 7 was the fact that the march was illegal. Circuit Court Judge James Hare of Dallas County, which included Selma, had issued an injunction on July 9, 1964, that threatened to shut down Alabama's civil rights movement entirely. It forbade people with ties to activist leaders from SNCC, SCLC, and other activist organizations to gather in groups of more than three. Hare's court

FIGHTING BACK BACKFIRES

Annie Lee Cooper fought back when she was attacked by Sheriff Jim Clark.

Television viewers witnessed an uncommon event at Selma's courthouse: a protester struck back. Annie Lee Cooper, whose white employer had fired her in 1963 for participating in Freedom Day, again stood among the protesters at the courthouse on January 25, 1965. "Nobody's afraid of them," she said out loud as police harassed protesters. Sheriff Jim Clark shoved her violently. When she protested, he slapped her. Cooper punched him in the face several times. Clark clubbed her on the head.

Television cameras zoomed in on the violence. The recordings made her look like a troublemaker, not a victim, wrote media historian Aniko Bodroghkozy. Viewers got "a jostled and obstructed view of the woman on the ground being handcuffed as numerous photographers and cameramen surround the action,

cutting to a bizarre extreme close-up of the woman. . . . She was either smiling or grimacing; it was hard to tell which." CBS broadcast the film on its nightly news report. In an interview, Clark explained that he was simply trying to bring order. Viewers never heard Cooper's side—she was not interviewed.

Activists knew the risks of demonstrating with television audiences watching. For this reason, organizers of the 1963 march in Washington, D.C., had reminded protesters that "demonstrating with discipline and dignity by their very presence will create great sympathy with our objectives." They also warned "that any disorder, any disruption, will be tragic precisely because at this moment it may well turn public opinion against all we stand for."

order gave law enforcement permission to break up gatherings of civil rights protesters.

King had second thoughts about the March 7 protest. Television viewers watching protesters calmly cross the bridge had no idea the march had begun with confusion. King was busy in Atlanta and had tried to delay the march. But hundreds already packed Brown Chapel. Outrage simmered over Jackson's death, the abuse of protesters at the courthouse, and centuries of being denied the ballot. An organizer later explained, "You never get people that ready, and don't do nothing. . . . We had to march in some form or fashion that day, to keep from killing the movement. We called Dr. King and told him what the situation was and we explained to him why we had to walk." Williams won a coin toss among SCLC leaders in Selma to take King's place. Lewis marched next to him, not as a SNCC representative but as an individual devoted to the cause.

There was no stopping the cameramen either. Lewis pointed out that Pierce and other cameramen "could have just skipped the whole thing. Or he could have just shot what was safe, what the authorities wanted him to shoot. But he didn't. None of them did, not the good ones . . . they went after the truth and showed America what was really happening." Their films had the effect of bringing the civil rights struggle into the homes of every American.

State troopers used clubs and tear gas against the nonviolent Selma marchers.

Broadcasts of Bloody Sunday moved people to action. Demonstrations in support of Selma civil rights activists took place in more than 80 U.S. cities, including outside the White House. Inside the Capitol, some congressmen gave speeches comparing Governor Wallace to Adolf Hitler and Clark's deputies to Hitler's Nazi troops.

ChapterFour
MONTGOMERY AT LAST

Television viewers saw Clark's mounted men race onto the bridge on the day that became known as Bloody Sunday. Deputies clubbed panicked marchers fleeing into downtown Selma. Inside Brown Chapel almost 100 marchers with bruises, bleeding wounds, broken teeth, jaws, arms, and legs filled the floor and pews. Some lay unconscious. Outside the church, police gathered. Angry black youths threw bottles and bricks at the police while some adults discussed fetching guns to get even. But the SCLC leader Andrew Young urged them to be practical: They could not defeat Clark's armed men. The marchers would soon learn that television recordings of the attack were more powerful weapons than guns would have been.

Determined activists planned another march to Montgomery for Tuesday, March 9. But marchers needed protection. Montgomery-born civil rights lawyer Fred Gray stepped in. He had argued before the Supreme Court that Tuskegee, Alabama, city officials drew city borders to prevent black residents from voting. On Monday, March 8, Gray asked U.S. District Judge Frank M. Johnson to stop state troopers from interfering with the next march. Meanwhile, Governor Wallace's representatives

insisted that another march would endanger the public. Civil rights leaders trusted Judge Johnson. He had ordered the Ku Klux Klan to stop abusing Freedom Riders. He was also the first judge to order Alabama counties to allow black people to register. But he needed more information to decide if another march would be safe. He ordered the march delayed.

By Tuesday afternoon, protesters—including volunteers from 30 states—packed Brown Chapel. They were excuted and nervous about what they were about to do. King knew that canceling the march

Marchers knelt to pray during the day that became known as "Turnaround Tuesday."

would cause disappointment, even outrage and chaos. Along with SNCC activist Forman and other civil rights leaders, King led the mile-long column of 1,500 marchers toward the Edmund Pettus Bridge. The same arrangement of armed men awaited—with 500 more state troopers than on Sunday.

But the real surprise was yet to come. Major Cloud, who was once again in charge of state troopers, ordered the marchers to halt. The marchers knelt to pray. But this time, there was no attack. Cloud ordered, "Troopers, withdraw. Clear the road completely—move out." King found himself in an awkward position: If he led marchers forward, he would break Judge Johnson's order. King had never before gone against a federal court order. The success of this campaign would depend on support from the federal government's courts, Congress, and President Johnson. He would need the support. King instructed the marchers to retreat. Brown Chapel soon filled—not with wounded marchers—but with angry, disappointed ones. King tried to calm them with the promise of another march.

But the story of "Turnaround Tuesday" was not over. On a dark street that night, a group of white men attacked three white ministers who had traveled from Boston to march. One of them, 38-year-old James Reeb, suffered a skull fracture. His wife was interviewed on TV just before he died as a result of it. Reeb's death further outraged caring people throughout the nation.

Inside Montgomery's federal courthouse on March 15, Judge Johnson listened to victims of Bloody Sunday describe what happened, and then the lights went off. Three minutes of Pierce's film played. John Lewis remembered that "when the courtroom lights were turned back on, Judge Johnson stood silently, shook his head, straightened his robe, and called for a recess. He was visibly disgusted. . . . From his demeanor, I just knew he was going to rule for us."

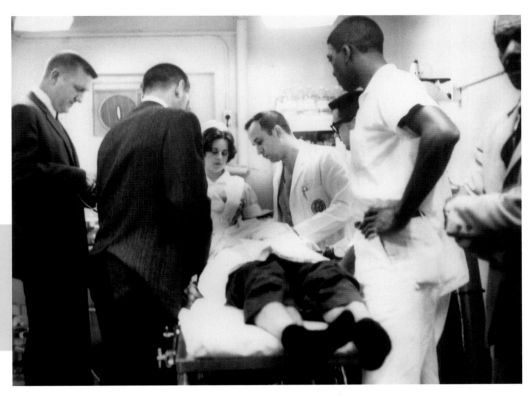

Doctors did their best but were unable to save James Reeb after he was brutally attacked by anti–civil rights Alabamans.

Activists had gained another powerful ally. That evening TV networks broadcast live from the Capitol, where President Johnson addressed Congress. Lewis and King watched from Selma along with 70 million viewers. King and the president had privately agreed that a voting rights bill was necessary. The president had resisted moving as quickly as King urged—until the shock of Bloody Sunday.

Now Congress members and television viewers heard Johnson explain that the nation's democracy could not survive without a voting rights bill. He said, "What happened in Selma is part of a far larger movement which reaches into every section and state of America. It is the effort of American Negroes to secure for themselves the full blessings of American life. Their cause must be our cause too. Because it is not just Negroes, but really it is all of us, who must overcome the crippling legacy of bigotry and injustice." Then Johnson echoed the motto of the civil rights movement: "And we shall overcome." In Selma, Lewis glimpsed King wipe away tears. Television cameras in the nation's Capitol showed Congress members rising to their feet to applaud, though many from the South did not.

Judge Johnson granted permission for another march. President Johnson announced that he would send thousands of military police and army troops to protect marchers all the way to Montgomery.

On Sunday, March 21, marchers set out from Brown Chapel for a third time. Army helicopters circled above and jeeps followed. Even if troops protecting marchers harbored racist attitudes, they were "forced by the cameras to be on their best behavior as they accompanied the marchers through the city streets," wrote historian Gary May in *Bending Toward Justice*. A truck escorted the marchers, carrying television lights and busy crews.

Television cameras filmed Hosea Williams and Lewis in the front of the line marching with protest organizers James Forman and A. Philip Randolph. However, those behind were not forgotten. Lewis later explained, "We were all very sensitive about this,

"Their cause must be our cause too. Because it is not just Negroes, but really it is all of us, who must overcome the crippling legacy of bigotry and injustice."

The aerial view of those marching across the Edmund Pettus Bridge was taken by a local newspaper.

about keeping the focus as much as possible on the people who had brought this historic day about, the everyday men and women of Selma. We made a point to put them at the front of the march, right behind the row that led the way." King invited Amelia Boynton to join them at the front of the line. Jimmie Lee Jackson's 82-year-old grandfather marched to Montgomery too.

Looking down on the marchers from the crest of the Edmund Pettus Bridge, C.T. Vivian marveled at "that long line, so wide and big and beautiful . . . It was celebration." Beyond Selma, black residents along the route cheered and brought the marchers food and drinks. Some joined the march. The night before the marchers arrived in Montgomery, famous musicians, comedians, and actors arrived to perform and transform the camp into an outdoor festival.

But mixed emotions filled the marchers as they approached Montgomery's state Capitol on March 25. They saw the Confederate flag waving alongside the state flag. The march leaders knew that racism and violence were always nearby in Alabama. Several wore the same blue suit as King to confuse assassins. The danger was real: By that night, another protester would be dead.

TV networks broadcast live from Montgomery as King spoke to marchers, now numbering more than 25,000 people. He knew they were

NEVER FORGET SELMA

Transferring old, taped footage into today's digital format is a time-consuming, but important, process.

One way we remember the Selma marches is by the rolls of 16mm film that cameramen used to record those events. Each roll of film in their cameras could record about 11 minutes of action. Editors connected these long strips and cut them apart in different places to tell the stories for TV audiences. These valuable pieces of film, like museum treasures, must be stored in cool vaults and handled with special gloves to avoid damage.

But news film has not often been treated with such care. For example, one major television station in Montgomery, Alabama—the place where massive civil rights protests began—no longer has any of its news films from the 1950s or 1960s because someone threw them all away in the early 1970s. NBC archives contain the unedited films from that time period but not the edited news stories broadcast on its nightly news program. CBS held on to its films of the Selma campaign, but they were so scratched and dusty that they needed cleaning and repair before they could be used in the 2014 movie *Selma*. To preserve the images on these fragile films, they are scanned into digital formats that can be easily shared and viewed again and again.

exhausted, their feet aching. He told them they were unstoppable. Racism had not stopped their progress to Montgomery and it would not stop their struggle for justice and equality. Governor Wallace never appeared, though he did watch from his office.

That night, television delivered terrible news. Thirty-nine-year-old Viola Liuzzo from Detroit, Michigan, had marched to Montgomery. The white activist was shot to death by KKK members as she drove fellow marchers, who were black, back to Selma. President Johnson himself announced the arrests of suspects on television.

"It's everybody's fight," Liuzzo had explained to her family before leaving for Selma. President Johnson believed it was his fight too. The voting rights bill made slow but steady progress through Congress. The same states that resented the federal government's control during Reconstruction now resented its involvement in their voting practices. But more Congress members were in favor of the new laws.

Less than five months after Bloody Sunday, television cameramen and civil rights leaders gathered in the office in which Lincoln had signed the Emancipation Proclamation abolishing slavery. They witnessed Johnson signing the Voting Rights Act into law on August 6, 1965. The new legislation banned literacy tests and poll taxes. It also targeted Alabama,

State troopers stood across the road from the car in which Viola Liuzzo was murdered.

Mississippi, other southern states, and some northern and western states with a history of discriminating against black applicants. Federal registrars would oversee voter registration there. These states needed federal approval before changing any voting procedure. The federal government's attorney general could now sue states for voter discrimination.

Lewis would recall this time as the end of a chapter: The nonviolent movement was losing younger activists. In coming years these activists would call for a new, militant attitude in the fight for equal rights. Lewis understood "people not wanting to get beaten anymore." But he never lost faith in nonviolent protest—and the power of cameras and journalists. "If it hadn't been for the media—the print media and television—the civil rights movement would have been like a bird without wings, a choir without a song," Lewis once said. By the end of 1965, 250,000 new black voters had registered. In Mississippi only 7 percent of registered voters were black in 1964. Five years later 67 percent of voters were black. In 1972 Andrew Young and Barbara Jordan became the first black southerners elected to Congress since Reconstruction.

Lewis himself was elected to Congress in 1987, representing Georgia for more than three decades. When Barack Obama was elected president in 2008, Lewis marveled: "When we were organizing voter-registration drives, going on the Freedom Rides, sitting in, coming here to Washington for the first time, getting arrested, going to jail, being beaten, I never thought—I never dreamed—of the possibility that an African American would one day be elected president of the United States."

"If it hadn't been for the media— the print media and television— the civil rights movement would have been like a bird without wings, a choir without a song."

MARCHING ONWARD

President Barack Obama and first lady Michelle Obama joined with John Lewis and Amelia Boynton on a march to the Edmund Pettus Bridge to mark the 50th anniversary of Bloody Sunday.

On the 50th anniversary of Bloody Sunday, thousands of marchers crossed the Edmund Pettus Bridge with the nation's first black president. Barack Obama held the hands of 103-year-old Amelia Boynton and 75-year-old John Lewis. Unlike the grainy black-and-white film of the attack 50 years earlier, TV viewers in 2015 saw this event live and in full color. At the foot of the bridge, President Obama said, "If Selma taught us anything, it's that our work is never done. . . . We know the march is not yet over. We know the race is not yet won."

Laws across the country still make it challenging for some people to vote. In 2013 the Supreme Court ruled in *Shelby County v. Holder* that "preclearance" was no longer necessary since black and white citizens were voting at the same rates in the states with a history of voter discrimination. But Justice Ruth Bader Ginsburg disagreed. In her dissent, she wrote, "Throwing out preclearance when it has worked and is continuing to work to stop discriminatory changes is like throwing away your umbrella in a rainstorm because you are not getting wet." Some state laws make voting more challenging by opening voting places less often, closing down voting places in black districts, or requiring a government-issued identification card, for example.

Timeline

1870

The 15th Amendment to the Constitution is ratified, granting black male citizens the right to vote.

1930

Mahatma Gandhi leads a three-week march to the shores of the Arabian Sea to collect salt and protest harsh British rule and its unjust salt tax.

1941

Civil rights leader A. Philip Randolph planned a march on Washington, D.C., to protest segregation in the military. To avoid this march, President Roosevelt negotiated a settlement with him.

1957

The Civil Rights Act of 1957, the first major legislation to protect civil rights since Reconstruction, gives the federal government authority to sue people who prevent any citizen from voting.

1960

The Civil Rights Act of 1960 is designed to strengthen the Civil Rights Act of 1957. Federal officials are appointed to inspect voting practices in the South.

1944

Civil rights lawyer Thurgood Marshall wins *Smith v. Allwright*—the Supreme Court rules that it is unconstitutional for the Southern Democratic Party to bar black voters from voting in primary elections.

1954

The Supreme Court rules in *Brown v. Board of Education* that segregation in public schools is unconstitutional.

1955

Civil rights activist Rosa Parks is arrested in Montgomery, sparking the first major massive protest of the civil rights movement. Dr. Martin Luther King Jr. is a major organizer of the yearlong boycott.

1963

Thousands participate in the March on Washington in support of the Civil Rights bill. SNCC chairman John Lewis is the youngest speaker there.

July 2, 1964

The Civil Rights Act of 1964 passes and makes segregation illegal in public places.

Summer 1964

Freedom Summer, a massive drive by several civil rights groups, takes place in Mississippi to register black voters with the help of white volunteers from the North.

Timeline

August 1964

The Mississippi Freedom Democratic Party takes the floor at the Democratic National Convention in New Jersey to demand participation. Activist Fannie Lou Hamer speaks on live television.

January 2, 1965

Martin Luther King Jr. launches the "Give us the ballot!" campaign in Selma's Brown Chapel.

February 18, 1965

Activist Jimmie Lee Jackson is shot during a demonstration in Marion, Alabama, and dies eight days later.

March 21, 1965

Civil rights leaders from several organizations lead marchers on a four-day journey to Montgomery with the protection of the federal government.

March 25, 1965

Marchers arrive in Montgomery, where Martin Luther King Jr. delivers a speech to the protesters. Activist Viola Liuzzo is murdered that night.

2006

Congress approves the extension of the Voting Rights Act for 25 years.

March 7, 1965

John Lewis, Hosea Williams, and local activists lead the first attempted march to Montgomery that ends in the violence of Bloody Sunday.

March 9, 1965

Martin Luther King Jr. joins march leaders in a second attempted march to Montgomery that ends with a retreat to Brown Chapel on this Turnaround Tuesday. Activist James Reeb is murdered that night.

2013

The Supreme Court rules in *Shelby County v. Holder* that preclearance is no longer necessary since black and white citizens are voting at the same rates in the states with a history of voter discrimination.

2015

President Barack Obama joins John Lewis, Amelia Boynton, and other civil rights leaders and marchers to cross the Edmund Pettus Bridge and commemorate the 50th anniversary of Bloody Sunday.

Glossary

appall—to overcome with shock or dismay

amendment—a formal change to a law or legal document, such as the U.S. Constitution

ballot—paper or mechanical methods used to record a vote

boycott—to refuse to buy or use a product or service to protest something believed to be wrong or unfair

civil rights—rights to equal treatment granted by law to every citizen of a country

delegate—a person elected to do a task for a group, such as casting a vote

demonstration—a gathering of people who want to show that they support or oppose something

deputy—someone with permission to act on behalf of an authority

discrimination—unfair treatment of people because of race, religion, gender, sexual preference, or age

footage—film or video recorded with images of an event

injunction—a written court order forbidding an action from taking place

jury—a group of people chosen to make a decision based on facts presented in court

literacy—the ability to read and write

polling station—a place where people vote

primary—an election where candidates are chosen by the major political parties before an election

Reconstruction—the process of rebuilding southern states after the Civil War and bringing them back into the Union (1865–1877)

registrar—a person who keeps official records

segregation—laws that keep people of different races, religions, ethnic groups or genders, separate from each other

Additional Resources

Further Reading

Aretha, David. *The Story of the Selma Voting Rights Marches in Photographs.* Berkeley Heights, NJ: Enslow Publishing, 2014.

Burgan, Michael. *The Voting Rights Act of 1965.* North Mankato, MN: Capstone Press, 2015.

Lewis, John, and Andrew Aydin. *March: Book Three.* Marietta, GA: Top Shelf Productions, 2016.

Weatherford, Carole Boston. *Voice of Freedom: Fannie Lou Hamer, Spirit of the Civil Rights Movement.* Somerville, MA: Candlewick Press, 2015.

Internet Sites

Selma Bridge Crossing Jubilee
https://www.selma50.com/mission-history

Selma to Montgomery Marches
https://www.nationalgeographic.org/news/selma-montgomery-marches-and-1965-voting-rights-act/

Teaching for Change
https://www.teachingforchange.org/selma-bottom-up-history

Critical Thinking Questions

King invited Amelia Boynton to walk with the leaders of the third march. How did local civil rights leaders and leaders of national organizations like SCLC and SNCC depend on each other?

For King and other leaders, violence was a critical part of nonviolent protest. Do you think the Voting Rights Act of 1965 could have been passed without the terrible violence on the Edmund Pettus Bridge? Use examples from the text to support your answer.

Journalists wrote detailed descriptions of what they saw on Bloody Sunday. Roy Reed in *The New York Times* wrote, "The troopers rushed forward. . . . The first 10 or 20 [marchers] were swept to the ground screaming. . . . A cheer went up from the white spectators lining the south side of the highway. The mounted possemen spurred their horses and rode at a run into the retreating mass." Compare the experiences of reading about the event to watching the film recording. Compare the kind of information each provides. Also, compare how each creates an impact on the viewer or reader. Which do you think is more effective?

Source Notes

p. 6, "There was no singing, no shouting… you could hear…" John Lewis. *Walking With the Wind*. New York: Simon and Schuster, 1998, pp. 325-326.

p. 9, "Never…" Sheriff Jim Clark, Segregationist Icon, Dies at 84," Associated Press, June 6, 2007, http://www.nbcnews.com/id/19075327/ns/us_news-life/t/sheriff-jim-clark-segregationist-icon-dies/#.WsWyxYjwbIU Accessed August 9, 2018.

p. 9, "one of the most gratifying and most memorable moments of my whole life…" "Determining the Facts," NPR, https://www.nps.gov/nr/twhp/wwwlps/lessons/133semo/133facts2.htm Accessed August 9, 2018.

p. 10, "Oh my god, how many people did I lead to their death today?" Ibid., Accessed August 9, 2018.

p. 10, "somber and subdued, almost like a funeral procession…" Ibid., Accessed August 9, 2018.

p. 11, "This is an unlawful assembly…" *Walking With the Wind*, pp. 326–327.

p. 12, "We should kneel and pray… Troopers, advance! People are going to die here…" Ibid., p. 328.

p. 13, "remember anything else, except the pictures that I saw and what was told to me…" Ibid.

p. 14, "I think I got it. I mean I hope I got it. I feel like I got it…" Gary May, "50th Anniversary of Bloody Sunday," Duke University Press online, https://dukeupress.wordpress.com/2015/03/06/50th-anniversary-of-bloody-sunday/0 Accessed August 9, 2018.

p. 14, "There was no way print could capture the drama and the vicious attack on the demonstrators on "Bloody Sunday" the way TV did…" "Selma and Richard Valeriani: A Reporter's Story," December 6, 2017, https://www.huffingtonpost.com/nancy-doyle-palmer-/selma-and-richard-valeria_b_6414664.html Accessed August 9, 2018.

p. 15, "all faced danger, especially the TV guys, who were easily identified and easy targets because of their equipment… Pierce, in particular…" *Walking With the Wind*, p 268.

p. 17, "got to really gear up, get our stuff organized, organize the community, … to Montgomery!" https://snccdigital.org/events/bloody-sunday/

p. 17, "a shrill cry of terror, unlike any sound that had passed…describe the motions…" George B. Leonard, "Midnight Plane to Alabama," May 4, 2008, https://www.thenation.com/article/midnight-plane-alabama/ Accessed August 9, 2018.

p. 17, "When Bloody Sunday was televised all over the country, today you would say it went viral…" Bryan Henry, "California woman travels to Selma to remember 'Bloody Sunday,'" Raycom Media, 2015, http://raycomgroup.worldnow.com/story/28275850/california-woman-travels-to-selma-to-remember-bloody-sunday Accessed August 9, 2018.

p. 20, "15th Amendment in flesh and blood…" "The Fifteenth Amendment in Flesh and Blood: The Symbolic Generation of Black Americans in Congress, 1870–1887," History, Art & Archives, United States House of Representatives, http://history.house.gov/Exhibitions-and-Publications/BAIC/Historical-Essays/Fifteenth-Amendment/Introduction/ Accessed August 9, 2018.

p. 21, "Without the ballot, you have no citizenship, no status, no power in this country…" *Bending Toward Justice*, p xiii.

p. 24, "And I felt like he was talking to me…" "Rep. John Lewis on the Need for Congress to Act Now on Gun Violence and Mass Shootings," June 22, 2016, Congressman John Lewis homepage, https://johnlewis.house.gov/media-center/press-releases/rep-john-lewis-need-congress-act-now-gun-violence-and-mass-shootings Accessed August 9, 2018.

p. 25, "Television pictures of recurring horrors such as the attacks that bloodied Freedom Riders…" Richard Pearson, "Veteran Newscaster Howard K. Smith Dies," *Washington Post*, February 19, 2002, https://www.washingtonpost.com/archive/local/2002/02/19/veteran-newscaster-howard-k-smith-dies/02c356b9-30d4-4df3-b621-8a4bc98b6400/?utm_term=.37d177394478 Accessed August 8, 2018.

p. 26, "We knew their theory was nonviolence, so we base our theory on nonviolence also. This has stunned them. They were expecting police brutality…" Aniko Bodroghkozy. *Equal Time: Television and the Civil Rights*, Chicago: University of Illinois Press, 2013, p 5.

p. 26, "Down here we make our own law…"

Gene Roberts, and Hank Klibanoff. *The Race Beat: The Press, the Civil Rights Struggle, and the Awakening of a Nation*. New York: Vintage Press, September 4, 2007 (ebook), location 5516.

p. 28, "As it stands now…for lack of a sixth grade education…" Lauren Feeney, "Two Versions of John Lewis' Speech, Moyers & Company, July 24, 2013, https://billmoyers.com/content/two-versions-of-john-lewis-speech/Accessed August 9, 2018.

p. 29, "If the Mississippi Freedom Democratic Party is … human beings in America?" Henry J. Perkinson. *Getting Better: Television & Moral Progress*. New York: Routledge, 2017, excerpts, https://snccdigital.org/people/fannie-lou-hamer/ and https://books.google.com/books?id=niNHDwAAQBAJ&pg=PT61&lpg=PT61&dq=television+coverage+mississippi+missing+chaney&source=bl&ots=_I0BLdKc-B&sig=zJptwavYZEMl5-m6nNHSST9Xqfw&hl=en&sa=X&ved=2ahUKEwj6yMyq7r3aAhUKPN8KHdYpAHo4ChDoATAHegQIABBP#v=onepage&q=television%20coverage%20mississippi%20missing%20chaney&f=false Accessed August 9, 2018.

p. 29, "token seats, in the back row, the same as we got in Mississippi. We didn't come all this way for that mess again…" Ibid., Accessed August 9, 2018.

p. 32, "Sheriff Jim Clark was a big man … but also white citizens…" "Determining the Facts," NPR, https://www.nps.gov/nr/twhp/wwwlps/lessons/133semo/133facts2.htm Accessed August 9, 2018.

p. 36, "Don't you have enough trouble of your own in…got a little too quiet for me…" *Bending Toward Justice*, p 75.

p. 37, "It was a small incident. One Negro fell down…" *Equal Time*, p. 126.

p. 38, "The blood of Jackson will be on our hands … to sleep on the highways…" *Bending Toward Justice*, p. 81.

p. 39, "In a crisis, we must have a sense of drama…" Ibid., p. 67.

p. 40, "Nobody's afraid of them…" Ibid., pp. 64–65.

p. 40, "a jostled and obstructed view of the woman on the ground being handcuffed as numerous photographers and cameramen…" *The Race Beat*, location 9092.

p. 40, "demonstrating with discipline and dignity…" *Equal Time*, p. 101.

p. 41, "You never get people that ready, and don't do nothing..." "Determining the Facts," NPR, https://www.nps.gov/nr/twhp/wwwlps/lessons/133semo/133facts2.htm Accessed August 9, 2018.

p. 41, "could have just skipped the whole thing," *Walking With the Wind*, p. 268.

p. 41, "the appalling silence and indifference of the good people..." *The Race Beat*, location 9092.

p. 45, "Troopers, withdraw. Clear the road completely..." Ibid., p. 103.

p. 46, "when the courtroom lights were turned back on, Judge Johnson stood silently, shook his head, straightened his robe, and called for a recess..." *Walking With the Wind*, p. 337.

p. 47, What happened in Selma is..." "President Johnson's Special Message to the Congress: The American Promise," LBJ Presidential Library, March 15, 1965, http://www.lbjlibrary.org/lyndon-baines-johnson/speeches-films/president-johnsons-special-message-to-the-congress-the-american-promise Accessed August 9, 2018.

p. 48, "forced by the cameras to be on their best behavior as they accompanied the marchers through the city streets..." *Bending Toward Justice*, p. 133.

p. 48, "We were all very sensitive about this, about keeping the focus as much as possible on the people who had brought this historic day about..." *Walking With the Wind*, p. 342.

p. 50, "that long line, so wide and big and beautiful. .." "Determining the Facts," NPR, https://www.nps.gov/nr/twhp/wwwlps/lessons/133semo/133facts2.htm Accessed August 9, 2018.

p. 50, "Yes, we are on the move and no wave of racism can stop us...no lie can live forever..." *Bending Toward Justice*, p. 14.

p. 54, "people not wanting to get beaten anymore..." *Walking With the Wind*, p. 347.

p. 54, "If it hadn't been for the media—the print media and television—the civil rights movement would have been like a bird without wings, a choir without a song..." *The Race Beat*, location 9725–9731.

p. 54, "When we were organizing voter-registration drives, going on the Freedom Rides, sitting in, coming here to Washington..." Biography.com, https://www.biography.com/people/john-lewis-21305903 Accessed August 9, 2018.

p. 55, "If Selma taught us anything, it's that our work is never done..." "Remarks by the President at the 50th Anniversary of the Selma to Montgomery Marches," The White House, Office of the Press Secretary, March 7, 2015, https://obamawhitehouse.archives.gov/the-press-office/2015/03/07/remarks-president-50th-anniversary-selma-montgomery-marches Accessed August 9, 2018.

p. 55, "Throwing out preclearance when it has worked and is continuing to work... "Voting Issues Today, Teaching Tolerance," https://www.tolerance.org/sites/default/files/general/Selma-TBTTB_voting_handout.pdf Accessed August 9, 2018.

Select Bibliography

Bodroghkozy, Aniko. *Equal Time: Television and the Civil Rights*. Chicago: University of Illinois Press, 2013.

Garrow, David. *Protest at Selma: Martin Luther King, Jr., and the Voting Rights Act of 1965.* New Haven: Yale University Press, 2015.

Lewis, John. *Walking With the Wind*. New York: Simon and Schuster, 1998.

May, Gary. *Bending Toward Justice: The Voting Rights Act and the Transformation of American Democracy*. New York: Basic Books, 2013.

Mudd, Roger. *The Place to Be: Washington, CBS, and the Glory Days of Television News*. New York: Public Affairs, 2008.

Roberts, Gene, and Hank Klibanoff. *The Race Beat: The Press, the Civil Rights Struggle, and the Awakening of a Nation*. New York: Vintage Press, 2007.

Index

About the Author

Danielle Smith-Llera taught children to think and write about literature in the classroom before turning to writing books for them. She wrote about the lunch counter sit-in protests for Capstone and is grateful for the opportunity to write about where the civil rights movement went from there. She will never take her right to vote for granted again!